Erasures of
My Coming Out
(Letter)

Mary Warren Foulk

First Place Winner of The Poetry Box Chapbook Prize, 2021

Editing & Book Design: Shawn Aveningo Sanders
Cover Layout/Typography: Shawn Aveningo Sanders
Cover Artwork: "Fluid Blocks" by Susan Allabashi
                (billingtondesigns.com/about)
Author Photo:Jay Miller-Foulk

ISBN: 978-1-956285-01-7
Printed in the United States of America.
Wholesale Distribution via Ingram.

Published by The Poetry Box®, February 2022
Portland, Oregon
ThePoetryBox.com

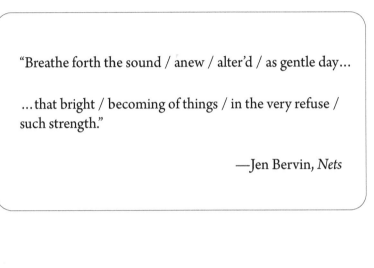

"Breathe forth the sound / anew / alter'd / as gentle day…

…that bright / becoming of things / in the very refuse /
such strength."

—Jen Bervin, *Nets*

Dear Mom,

There's something I need to share with you, that I've been keeping from you. I can't keep it in anymore. I am burdened by secrecy and the stress is weighing on me. I am sorry to be doing this by mail. For me, a letter is the most effective, the easiest and perhaps most considerate way to convey what I am thinking and feeling. I want you to know that I am with Alyson. She is not just my roommate, but also my partner and we have a wonderful, beautiful relationship and life together in New York. I've waited until now to tell you for a number of reasons—please trust and try to understand them.

I needed the time and space for my sake, to feel comfortable with and committed to me, my identity, my choices and needs, to feel comfortable with and committed to my relationship with Alyson. I know this is hard, it's not the "norm," especially for our family and family expectations. We're not the most liberal of families. And it's weird for me. It's difficult to be gay—society makes it so. I don't even necessarily identify as such. I feel as if I met this great person and I want to be with this great person. I know this will take some time to adjust to, to accept, for all involved. I was scared, scared of rejection, of more loss, disappointment, judgment. I know this is not what you would necessarily want or hope for me. I love and adore Alyson, she is phenomenal, incredibly special, and vital to me. I am not validating or respecting her or me, our choices, by being silent, hidden. I can't and don't want to deny us anymore. I want you to know me, fully. I don't want you to find out through some other means or after the fact.

Please don't respond right away. Take some time to read and re-read this, to think about your response, your feelings. I'm sorry it has taken me this long to tell you. It is my hope that we talk about this and over time, that you ask questions and tell me what you need. It is also my hope that you will get to know Alyson and that you will have the chance to see what I see.

Please always know that I love you.

Mary

Dear [   ],

There's something ▩▩▩▩▩▩▩▩▩▩▩▩▩▩ I've been keeping ▩▩
▩▩ I can't ▩▩▩▩▩▩▩▩▩▩▩▩▩▩▩▩▩▩▩▩▩▩▩▩

I can't

[   ]

Dear [   ],

burdened   secrecy

weighing

[   ]

Dear [   ],

a letter

to tell you

about

me

[   ]

DATE

Dear [   ],

—please

my sake, to feel comfortable
feel comfortable
this is hard

[   ]

Dear [   ],

difficult

to be gay—society

scared, scared

[   ]

Dear [   ],

rejection,   loss, disappointment,
this is not   hope

[   ]

Dear [   ],

I've
waited

my identity, my choices

silent,
hidden

this
long

[   ]

Dear [   ],

the stress

___

to adjust to

what

I am not

[   ]

Dear [   ],

this great person   this great person

not what you   want   for me

[   ]

Dear [   ],

family

most   families

society

you

deny us

[   ]

Dear [   ],

for a number of reasons—

the "norm"

is   you

your feelings

what you need.

[   ]

Dear [   ],

you

try

me

[   ]

Dear [   ],

I am sorry

I'm sorry

Mary

Dear [   ],

I

I   I

I

I   I

I

me, my   my

my

me

me. I

me.

I   me,

I

me, fully. I

me

my

me

I

Please   I

[   ]

Dear [   ],

I need

I am

I am

I am   I want

I know

I feel   I want
I know

I know   I love

I am

I want

I

see

I love

[   ]

Dear [   ],

not   roommate

[   ]

Dear [   ],

She   and we

together

us

about

we

[   ]

Dear [   ],

with Alyson.

Alyson,

Alyson

[   ]

Dear [   ],

_____ I _____
_____
_____
_____
_____ want _____
Alyson _____ my _____
_____ beautiful _____ life _____
_____
_____

_____
_____
_____
_____
_____
_____
_____
_____
_____
_____
_____
_____
_____

_____
_____
_____
_____
____

_____

[   ]

Dear [Alyson],

with you

I am

me.

I am me,

fully.

Mary

Dear [   ],

it

is

most considerate

to   trust

me   to

identify

me

validating

hope

and

love

[   ]

Dear [   ],

please understand

Please read and re-read think talk ask know see

Please

[   ]

Dear [   ],

family

society

you   have the chance

always

[   ]

Dear [   ],

most effective,

to tell

to tell
and tell

[   ]

Dear [   ],

a letter

is

not the "norm"

for me

anymore

[   ]

Dear [   ],

anymore

I don't
want

your

questions

[   ]

Dear [   ],

accept

me

[   ]

Dear [   ],

let

me

love (live)

[   ]

Dear [   ],

There's

me

a wonderful

gay—

fact.

Mary

Dear [   ],

beautiful

gay—

adore

fully

hope   and
                                hope

[   ]

Dear [   ],

beautiful

gay—

always   love you.

Mary

Note to the Reader

All poetry is fragment: it is shaped by its breakages, at every turn. It is the very art of turnings, toward the white frame of the page, toward the unsung, toward the vacancy made visible, that wordlessness in which our words are couched.

—Heather McHugh, *Broken English*

In this erasure collection, I am attempting a redaction, flipping the meaning of my coming out letter and the act itself on its head. I am highlighting and uncovering what formerly would have been hidden, silenced, challenged, and erased. I am making the text and meaning anew.

I was greatly influenced by the work of Jen Bervin and Mary Ruefle, among others. Assembling these poems and fragments, I referenced poet Ángel García's "Meditations on Erasures," in which he writes:

> *Erasure is language translated and retranslated. It makes meaning new. In this new language—code-switched (but not coded)—we are allowed to resist by expressing dissent. We are able to dismantle and deconstruct the official language. From the legacies of trauma, we can find power. Erasure is an assertion of that power. Erasure is recovery. Erasure is resistance. Erasure is resilience. Erasure is political will. Erasure is empowerment.*

Erasures can be viewed as both "an aesthetic and political act. Effacement, redaction, and illegibility...as tactics that artists can employ to combat, highlight, or heal sociopolitical invisibility." Erasures by people of color, disabled people, LGBTQ+ populations—communities rendered invisible, ESL, undocumented, women.

[. . .]

What if I never had to "come out"? What if I never had to write such a letter? What if the process was rendered unnecessary—erased? For some, it is unnecessary. For too many, it's costly. What might I have done with that energy if it hadn't been exerted on hiding, on passing, on fear, on denial? These are a few of the questions asked and answered.

—Mary Warren Foulk

Acknowledgments

I offer my love and gratitude to my wife, children, and extended family for their steadfast belief in me. Also, my deepest appreciation to Leslie Ullman for her transformative teaching and compassionate guidance. And to my close friends and invaluable editors—Pascale Giroux, Susan Allabashi, Kristy Bowen, Kate Senecal, and Siarra Riehl—as well as to my Vermont College of Fine Arts cohort for their ongoing encouragement and generous kindness. Lastly, my profound gratitude to The Poetry Box®, to Shawn Aveningo-Sanders and Robert Sanders, and to Judge Annie Lighthart for their remarkable support of my work. I am honored that *Erasures of My Coming Out (Letter)* found a home with them.

Praise for Erasures of My Coming Out (Letter)

To uncover the human heart that quietly waits inside every life and every poem is no small feat and yet is what *Erasures of My Coming Out (Letter)* does with deftness and hope. Shaped by both the weight of secrecy and the release of recovery, the poems draw our eyes and minds into the page and the careful search taking place in, around, and beneath each word. "Erasure poetry" may sound like it is the rubbing out of meaning, but the poems within this beautiful volume show that it has the very opposite effect, allowing love and truth to surface and catch the light that is their birthright.

—Annie Lighthart, Contest Judge, 2021
author of *PAX* and *Iron String*

Mary Warren Foulk's *Erasures of My Coming Out (Letter)* is an invitation, not only to experience the repetitive, exasperating nature of coming out, but also to experience coming into oneself. Foulk's poetry holds the roots of connection and understanding in its palms and offers them piecemeal to everyone who is willing to listen. Not only are the erasures in this collection moving, in every sense of the word, but also painfully necessary—today, tomorrow, always.

—Siarra Riehl, MFA
transdisciplinary novelist, teacher, and performer

Erasures of My Coming Out (Letter) is a true gift to the literary world, a fierce tour of the wild, nuanced gamut of the human emotional experience. Through poems that are so sparse they give the illusion of delicacy, Foulk demands space for her true self to bloom,

[. . .]

shines light into both the darkest and tidiest corners of living and therefore, by extension offers her findings to everyone else who needs them. These poems defy fragility, are frank in their calling out the injustice of circumstances that even demand a coming out letter through the reclamation, the recasting, the redefinition of the self, and with love. This manuscript is an unequivocal triumph.

—Kate Senecal, MFA, award-winning writer
Asst. Director of Pioneer Valley Writers' Workshop

This striking series of erasures plumbs the nature of redactions. Of the space between the words we write and the words we feel. Their bare, raw nature. Foulk's reworkings of her own language are stunning, and while it is fundamentally a coming out letter, it is also an invitation to be worked and reworked. A struggle toward meaning and family within language itself.

—Kristy Bowen, editor, dancing girl press

About the Author

Mary Warren Foulk has been published in *VoiceCatcher, Cathexis Northwest Press, Yes Poetry, Arlington Literary Journal* (Gival Press), *Los Angeles Poet Society, Pine Hills Review, Palette Poetry, Visitant, Silkworm,* and *Steam Ticket* among other publications. Her work also has appeared in *(M)othering Anthology* (Inanna Publications) and *My Loves: A Digital Anthology of Queer Love Poems* (Ghost City Press). Her chapbook, *If I Could Write You a Happier Ending,* is forthcoming from dancing girl press (2021).

Mary has attended several writing workshops and conferences, including The Writers Studio and AWP events, as well as received several artist and educator grants, including from the National Endowment of the Humanities. She recently won the "Teach! Write! Play!" fellowship to the Martha's Vineyard Institute of Creative Writing and her poem "The Inventory of Fumbling" received first place honors. Her poem "portrait of a queer as a young boy" has been nominated for the 2021 *Best of the Net Anthology.* A graduate of the MFA Writing program at Vermont College of Fine Arts, Mary lives in western Massachusetts with her wife and two children. She is an educator, writer, and activist.

Instagram: @mwfoulk

www.facebook.com/mary.w.foulk

Twitter: @mwfoulk

The Poetry Box Chapbook Prize

The Poetry Box® Chapbook Prize is open to both established poets and emerging talent alike. The contest is open to poets residing in the United States and is open for submissions each year during the month of February. Find more information at ThePoetryBox.com.

2021 Winners:

Erasures of My Coming Out (Letter) by Mary Warren Foulk

Of the Forest by Linda Ferguson

Let's Hear It for the Horses by Tricia Knoll

2020 Winners:

The Day of My First Driving Lesson by Tiel Aisha Ansari

My Mother Never Died Before by Marcia B. Loughran

Off Coldwater Canyon by C.W. Emerson

2019 Winners:

Moroccan Holiday by Lauren Tivey

Hello, Darling by Christine Higgins

Falling into the River by Debbie Hall

2018 Winners:

Shrinking Bones by Judy K. Mosher

November Quilt by Penelope Scambly Schott

14: Antología del Sonoran by Christopher Bogart

Fireweed by Gudrun Bortman

CPSIA information can be obtained
at www.ICGtesting.com
Printed in the USA
LVHW070453030122
707693LV00004B/12